Prison Segmentation For Coaching Clubs

Rev. Mike Wanner

Table Of Contents

Introduction

I have already introduced Segmentation in previous books and will just reference it here. Segmentation can reshuffle the space utilization and put fewer people in more spaces around the clock.

The primary goal is to spread people out and allow a more relaxed and less threatening environment. Coincidentally the process can increase safety and security by reducing occupancy so when things happen anywhere; fewer people are involved.

Facilities can create a B shift and a C Shift that will offer great new freedom possibilities for prisoners. Being able to select patterns or tracks of further segmentation that carries opportunities will promote feelings of personal empowerment and peace.

Management that chooses to make some adjustments based on this idea could have stress reduction throughout, and prisoners who are at higher risk may be more readily separated from potential conflicts with others.

1 - Why I Am Writing This Book

The human dynamics of prison are very complicated, and there is a disconnect effect where the social nature of occupants is stifled. Safety and security are issues but so is the need for human nurture which could be the essential ingredient for rehabilitation.

I have not seen an abundance of success stories about rehabilitated prisoners. On the contrary, I know we have high levels of recidivism which could lead taxpayers to increased frustration, taxes and further deterioration of American families.

The nation as a whole is dramatically impacted by the high cost of incarceration, but there is no clear pathway to change. It seems that chemical dependency is the treatment of choice for many citizens and that is helping to keep the level of occupancy very high.

A subtle but growing human performance effort is the topic of coaching which could help a lot. I earlier wrote a book called *Prison Possibilities Correction Coaches: Concept* which offers Ideas for staff using coaching.

Here I would like to have segmented prisoners working on it as part of their self-work towards reentry.

About 2.3 Million prisoners lives and 2.7 million children of prisoners lives and another million or 2 spouses equals a whole lot of people who have a detriment because of the status quo. Let us change what we can. Coaching can make that real.

2 - What Is Coaching

Coaching is a style of dialogue where a person identified as a coach engages in a two-way conversation with a newbie or client interested in accomplishing a specific goal in a variety of fields. The novice may be called a "coachee."

The process may be done informally between two people where one has some experience with the concept and offers support to the other. Coaching may be like mentoring but is usually less specifically focused and more general or overall in integrating possibilities.

The term has roots in academia and sporting skills development. In more recent times it is used with many communications to help clients shift their perspectives and thereby discover optimal approaches to achieve their goals.

The application is applied now in all kinds of human development which may include medicine, wellness, health training, personal, professional, sport, social, family, political, spiritual dimensions and competency in any area you choose. The coaches can develop questioning techniques and thought development that intertwines with and overlaps many areas of human engagement.

Prisoners who get coached or have coaching skill may find it very useful when they prepare for reentry or as a career after they leave prison. In some places, there is little or no certification or licensing required to be a coach.

If you are considering the field, professional training and or membership in a coaching organization may prove advantageous.

If entering the field professionally, it would be wise to review local laws and rules about holding yourself out as a Coach. Standards and methods of training coaches can vary widely between coaching organizations. Some business coaches refer to themselves as consultants, a broader business relationship which may be more profitable but may also be more risk-laden and credential dependent.

Career coaching focuses on work and career and is like career counseling. Career coaching is not to be confused with life coaching, which concentrates on personal development.

I would recommend both Life Coaching, and Career Coaching be considered by prisoners seeking Reentry.

You may wish to develop over time a protocol for Reentry Coaching so you can embrace your experience and use it to help others.

Christian coaching is routine among religious organizations and churches. A Christian coach may not be a pastor or counselor, but you should be very clear about your credentials and your skills.

Co-coaching is a structured practice of coaching between peers with the goal of learning improved coaching techniques. Life coaching is the process of helping people identify and achieve personal goals.

Although life coaches may have studied some counseling psychology or related subjects, a life coach should not act as a therapist, counselor, or health care provider unless they have all needed credentials.

Psychological intervention lies outside the scope of the life coaching.

Care is needed to avoid challenges from professionals who feel you overstep and are guilty of malpractice.

Co-coaching and referring out when appropriate could help coaches avoid a lot of trouble.

3 - Coaching Club Concept

The idea here is to start moving towards personal development. Prison is a complex living environment, and it is less than optimal circumstances for individual growth.

Segmentation takes a giant step forward in blazing an environmental trail that can be a lot more conducive to personal self-analysis, goal setting, and planning.

In this little book, I will offer some ideas that prisoners can begin to develop so they can consider if coaching might have some value for them. I will start with some self-inventory questions and suggest they look for partners to invite them to work with on a scheduled preplanned basis.

The suggestions will also likely have homework so the effort can be demonstrably significant.

The plan would start with :

1. Pre-Prison Self-Analysis Criteria.

2. Diligence Awareness Requirements

3. Ethical Considerations

4. Commitment

5. Post-Prison Self-Analysis Criteria.

4 - Pre-Prison Self Analysis Criteria

Your History Questions to Consider

(If Blocked about a question, no worries – come back if and when you remember). Ask now and let your subconscious answer when it is ready and not before

Favorite Subjects In Grade School

1._____

2._____

Favorite Subject In High School

1._____

2._____

Before Age 18, what did you dream of Doing?

1._____

Did You try to do it? Comments_____

2._____

Did You try to do it? Comments?_____

What Did You Do Which People Said They Liked?

1._____

2._____

What About You Do You Like Most

1._____

2._____

What Did You Want To Do That You Couldn't?

1._____

2._____

What Did You Enjoy Then?

1._____

2._____

What Activities Made You Feel Alive with Energy?

1._____

2._____

What Special Skills (Gifts) Did You Have?

1._____

2._____

5 - Diligence Awareness Requirements

You have asked yourself some questions, and you felt the feelings that came up. By now, hopefully, you have processed the feelings and decided whether to answer those for yourself.

If you have answered less than 50% of the questions, now might be a good time to pause and revisit the ideas and then decide for yourself if you are ready to proceed or give up.

If you are not able to do 50% on your own, it may not be fair for you to ask others to work with you. Pausing is not a situation where you give up unless you entirely choose that.

Pausing is an opportunity to talk to yourself about your motivations and take the time to go deeper and see if you might learn something about the bumps in your road that are holding it all back. Fear not. Worry not.

You get to choose to work harder or not.

There is a word called discernment, which means that the adult you decides for themselves about what to do next. Please do not hide from your challenges but determine all the options that there are to go from where you are in your life to where you want to be.

If you are still stuck, then you might want to double down on **fearing not** and make a list of what is the worst that can happen. If you decide to proceed anyhow, consider writing a letter to the people you would like to be in the club with as to how and why they should choose to take a chance on you.

6 - Ethical Considerations

Everybody Is Human and Has:

Light
Darkness
Wisdom
Fear
Uncertainty
Smarts
Defects
Dummy Tendencies
Occasional Daftness
Brilliance
Stupidity
All other good possibilities
All other bad options
Goals
Bad Stuff
More Good Stuff

Know:

You can help people no one else can.
You can be helped if you listen and discern.

14

7 - Commitment

Pledge Your Attention & Discernment

Some Things to Consider Including:

Acknowledge The Group Is A Choice:
1. Only Two Out Of Three Candidates May be Accepted
2. Best Efforts Matter
3. Values Really Matter
4. Prejudice of Any Kind is Unacceptable
5. Everyone Will be Rejected Once or More

The Importance of Respect You Have for The Group

Dedication to Listening & Hearing Others

Promise to Write Down and Share Only with Them
Exactly What You Heard Them Say and Ask For

Pledge to Vote Discreetly and Independently for The
Candidates Who Present And Are Ready to Apply

Your Willingness To Contribute

You Will Listen More Than Share

You Are Patient

You Will Wait Until You Are Eligible

You Will Learn Each Meeting

15

8 - Post-Prison Planning

Your Wish List To Do Soon

(If Blocked about a question, no worries – come back if and when you decide.) Ask now and Expect a Revelation.

Favorite Dreams?

1._____

2._____

Follow Up With A Family Plan?

1._____

2._____

What Is The Priority For Your Life?

1._____

2._____

What Do You Do Now That People Like?

1._____

2._____

What "You" Do You Like Most?

1._____

2._____

What Do You Want To Do That You Couldn't?

1._____

2._____

What Special Skills (Gifts) Do You Have?

1._____

2._____

What Do You Want to Do For Others?

1._____

2._____

What Activities Made You Feel Alive with Energy?

1._____

2._____

9 - Natural Coaching Tools

Listen Twice as Much as You Talk

"We have two ears and one mouth so that we can listen twice as much as we speak."
Attributed to Greek Philosopher Epictetus

Let's Build On That Ratio

Two Coach Want-to-Bees and One Being Coached

Everybody Can Learn in This Club

You Can Talk Up Possibilities

You Can Raise Ideals & Vibrations

You Can Invite Emotional Pain Release

You Can Help People by Caring & Listening & Understanding

10 - Coach Club Plan Meeting

Meet with the others in segmentation who have chosen to be segmented to participate in coaching club. Make sure that those you meet with have done their homework.

Everybody should have done at least their Pre-Prison Self-Analysis Criteria. Have a talk about everybody's progress and when you will be ready to start your meetings.

The primary goal of a coaching session is to listen to others and allow them to feel that they are being heard. You will likely be tempted to answer the issues they may be talking about, but that is not the goal of coaching.

Coaching is different than counseling in that the coach primarily listens and sometimes ask questions but avoids lecturing and telling the speakers what to do.

Coaching Questions have power by being targeted so that the speakers are asked for the answers in a way that is not threatening. The coach is not the authority, the speaker is.

Listeners can make notes so that they can create meaningful questions that smooth the process for the speaker.

Club members could create a schedule of their activities during the earliest meeting.

11 - Coach Club Member Note Pad

Your Coach Club Team-members Strengths Are:

_____

_____

_____

_____

_____

_____

_____

_____

_____

_____

_____

_____

_____

12 - Angel Help Is Available

Angel Raphael

The Angel of Healing - Archangel Raphael started my journey into writing about prisons. I had been writing early on in a series of messages that were later published as The Angel Raphael Speaks Series Volumes 1,2,3.

A prison minister I knew named Marion called to chat a bit about her mission in a women's prison. We talked, and all was well with the world and her ministry.

The very next morning I heard from Angel Raphael as was becoming usual and the first message about prison came through. Eventually, there would be only twenty-two messages total about jail that came through out of the three hundred or so in the entire series.

The message title was *Prison Life of the Future,* and I share the last two paragraphs of that message on Prison Life in the Future:

"Please consider as if the vibration of a prison existed on a scale that you could read called the love fear continuum. Consider that a single increment move on that scale that went away from fear and moved towards love was actually beneficial to all who passed through the premises.

As you ever so slightly held that thought, you entertained the possibility of a shift for the imprisoned and guards of the future. Congratulations, for you, have allowed some light to shine on a subject that is almost perpetually locked in pessimism." ARS 9 (Channeled about 80th in the Series) Angel Raphael is available to all. Invite him into your heart.

The first hundred or so messages from Angel Raphael are available free at http://angelraphaelspeaks.com/arsvo/ . After message set 10, Single Topic Message Set – Prisons has the first fourteen Prison Messages.

Angel Michael

Archangel Michael is known as the Angel of Protection and is a valuable resource to invite whenever you might need personal strength or protection.

Angel Gabriel

Archangel Gabriel is known as the Angel of Communication and is a valuable resource to invite whenever you need help writing or speak about the things that come into your awareness. Especially helpful Angel for those wanting better language skills. Precise language can have great value.

Other Angels

The Three Archangels above are well connected to millions of others. When you invite one or all, millions of others are on their teams and at your disposal. Remember to request God and Angels often, so you are connected and never feel vulnerable.

13 - The Wrap-up

I need to explain that this book is less direct than many I write and more invitational for readers to dip into possibilities. More than any other writing by me about prison, the readers are invited to take action to create the precise, unique steps necessary in their facility to choose the optimal options that make the impossible into real possibilities.

In coaching, the one being coached is the authority, and the coach is the servant of the process. I write all this in an entirely unusual format for application in a less than friendly environment; I know that you can help others and yourself through coaching.

I have given you here very little information about actual coaching, but the questions that you answer above can be incorporated into your personal database, so you know what you need to pursue. Resources abound about coaching; this book is an invitation to go look for them with the belief that they have a lot to offer you so you can provide a lot for the community that you will reenter.

Your calling to help others will help them and you. As you step up the ladder to success with others on your shoulders, you will not notice that you have broken significant obstacles that prevented you from believing you could once again find your right place in society as a favored child of the God Most High.

I invite you to choose segmentation, find your tribe, get the support you need as you support your tribe and serve people and God. May all who read this be blessed, AND SO IT IS!!!!!!

For
Considering
These
Ideas

Ever

It Does Not Help Prayer Still Does!

16 - Resource Books

Distant Healing Sessions (or Join Mail List) – Write To mikewann@voicenet.com

Books by Rev. Mike at **www.Amazon.com**

Veterans Healing Six Pack
1. *Trauma Healing Options for VA Hospitals: Help for Veterans to Own Their Healing and their future.*
2. *Trauma Healing Action Steps for Veterans: Help to Start Healing*
3. *Trauma Healing Action Steps for Veterans: Empowerment*
4. *Trauma Healing Action Steps for Veterans: Forgiveness*
5. *Trauma Healing Action Steps for Veterans: Thought Freedom*
6. *Tea For Veterans: Welcome One Home*

PTSD Power Pack:
1. *The PTSD Project: Turn Pain To Power*
2. *PTSD & Soul Retrieval: Putting One Back Together*
3. *PTSD & The Purple PAD: Calling all Scientists and PTSD Patients*

Angel Raphael Speaks Volume 1: Take Courage! God Has Healing in Store for You!
Angel Raphael Speaks Volume 2: Take Courage! God Has Healing in Store for You!
Angel Raphael Speaks Volume 3: Take Courage! God Has Healing in Store for You!
Angel Raphael Speaks Volume 4: Angels, Addicts, Alcoholics & Prisoners – Oh Yeah!
Angel Raphael Speaks Volume 5: Prisoners Caring for Alcoholics - Australia In Miniature Projects Intro
Angel Raphael Speaks Volume 6: Prisoners Caring for Addicts - Australia In Miniature For Addicts
Reiki Journaling from Japan
Reiki Is Alive: God's Great Gift
Four Parts to Healing
Distant Healing: We Are All Connected
Stress Release Energy Work: How To Cope
Does Reiki Love Heal Cancer?
Group Consciousness
Salute To Philadelphia VA Medical Center: Thank You
Reiki Transcript for Reiki 2 & 3 Channels: Dr. Usui Is That You?
God Bless Kindle & Amazon
Puppies Are Different From People
If Your Dog Dies
Toy Guns Are Obsolete

Great Spirit Made Children With Red Skin: AND
The Cage of Fear: Is Not Locked
God Made Children Red, Yellow, Brown, Black & White: Greet Each Child With Kindness
Emergency Medical Kindness In The Cradle Of Liberty: Big City - Cracked Bell
Angels Are Always Around Addicts and Addicts: Help Is Near Now! Invite It In!
Angels Are Always Around Addicts and Alcoholics: Volume 2 - Tools To Help Re-Light...
Prison Jobs Now: Providing Care For Addicts And Addicts
Controlled Care Communities Concept
Prison Possibilities Dialogue Series: Concept
Prison Possibilities Dialogue Series: Volume 2, 3, 4, 5 Dialogues
Prison Possibilities Voluntary Exile
Prison Possibilities Corrections Coaches
Prison Possibilities For Mexicans: Is A Boat Better Than A Wall?
Prison Possibilities Family Time: A Reason to Thrive!
Prison Genius Pool: "So Much Genius In Jail."
Prison Possibilities Access Control: Prisoner Access by Request
Prisoner's Lawyers Can Save The American Economy: Make A Buck Doing It & ...
Prisoner Family Talks, Days, Stays & Vacations: Connecting Helps Healing
Prisoner Writing Projects: Write To Heal, Start Over & Reconnect
Prison Cell Clearing & Blessing: Clear Entities, Chase Ghosts, & Create Sacred Space
Prisoner Professors: Show You Are Aware Create Change With Care
Prison Reiki? Maybe Someday? A Gateway To Help Heal Prisons & America?
Judges and An Angel Rule On Possibilities: We Can Cut Sentences & Prison Costs
Ideas For Prison Wardens: Leadership Is Not Easy
Solitary Community: Could Community Support Cut Costs and Issues?
Prison Project Communications Team: Communications Can Change Lives
Motivating & Empowering Prisoners? Invite Prisoners To Find Their Motivation
Prison Segmentation For Safety, And Sanity, Security, Peace, and Space
Prison Segmentation For Security
Dowsing for Prisoners; Answers from Above
Ex-Prisoner Possibilities With Real Estate Investors
Prison Segmentation For Joint Ventures
Prison Segmentation For Your Rehabilitation: R U Ready?
Prison Segmentation For Family Villages

Little Books at Kindle.com by Rev. Mike:
English Medical History Questionnaire For Non-English Speakers
English Language Helper For Non-English Speakers
Wise Wonderful Women Are The Well Of The Family
Answers for Test & Research: Dowsing Power
Crisis? Reiki! Baby? Reiki!
Bible References For Healing
Angel Raphael Speaks – Prisons
Angel Raphael Speaks – Veterans
The Saint Off Interstate 95

17 - Angels Please Prayers

Addict's

Angels of Healing Selected
Help Me to Stay Directed
Come To Me From The Sky
I Am Ready to Succeed Not Try
If I Don't Invite You In
I Might Not Win
I Have Been Lost For Too Long
Help Me To Stay Strong

Alcoholic's

Angels of Healing On High
Help Me to Stay Dry
Come To Me From The Sky
I Am Ready to Succeed Not Try
If I Don't Invite You In
I Might Not Win
I Have Been Lost For Too Long
Help Me To Stay Strong

From

http://AngelRaphaelSpeaks.com/AAAAAAA/

18 - Private Channeling

Angel Raphael Speaks a series of free messages that are channeled through Reverend Mike Wanner for the Highest good and Highest Healing of all concerned.

Many questions arise about Reverend Mike doing private channeling, and he does help with that so e-mail him.

Reverend Mike is available worldwide as a psychic channel, emotional release facilitator, spiritual energy practitioner & teacher, and public speaker. He looks forward to meeting you soon!

Email - mikewann@voicenet.com 215-342-1270 PRIVATE SPIRITUAL READINGS/channelings or Spiritual Healing Sessions: Telephone or in person. Rev. Mike is available for private, one-on-one intuitive sessions with you, his Guide Family, and your Guides. He helps by offering clarity on emotional situations about your life, your purpose, your spirituality, and the release of stuffed emotions and cellular memory.
Connect to the love of your Guides today!
Contact Rev. Mike for an appointment.

Sessions available:

Spiritual Readings
Angel Channeling
Distant Reiki Healing
Remote Clearing of Stuffed Emotions
Distant Clearing Cellular Memory
Distant Clearing Energy Blockages
Remote Clearing of the Chakras
Customized needs
Mastermind dowsing responses to yes/no direction finding questions.

Rev. Mike is a facilitator of healing. He brings you and the Divine together so that you can align with the Divine and have a great time and a great life. All healing is between you and God, as it should be. Go ahead and start without Rev. Mike. Visit his prayer site http://www.Create-A-Prayer.com. Take the first step NOW.

19 - Reverend Mike Wanner

Rev. Mike Wanner started his Metaphysical and Ministerial studies with Reiki in 1993 and had studied seven styles of Reiki in the U.S., Japan, Canada, Denmark and Australia. He is certified to teach. He became certified to teach Integrated Energy Therapy in 1999 and co-taught the first IET class of the new Millennium. Mike began dowsing in 2001.

Ordained as a Metaphysical Minister of the International Metaphysical Ministry and an Interfaith Minister of the Circle of Miracles Ministry, Rev. Mike practices and teaches spiritual energy therapies in the Philadelphia Area.

Rev. Mike holds ministerial degrees from the University of Metaphysics and the University of Sedona. He is a Pastoral Care Associate at Aria - Frankford Hospital. He taught at the National Academy of Massage Therapy and Health Sciences.

Rev. Mike was a faculty member of the Medical Mission Sister's Center for Human Integration's School of Integrated Body/Mind Therapies in Fox Chase, Philadelphia, PA for twelve years.

Rev. Mike is licensed by the teaching of Intuitional Metaphysics to practice Spiritual Healing and Scientific Prayer. Mike is also a Prayer therapist.

Rev. Mike was elected in 2007 to the status of "Fellow of the American Institute of Stress."

In 2008, Rev. Mike became a practitioner of Coincidental Recognition as he incorporated the CoRe System into his spiritual healing practice.

In 2009, Rev. Mike trademarked a new healing process called Quantum Quatro! Subtle Energy System Support®.

In 2011, Rev. Mike joined the outreach program known as the Health Advantage Group.

In 2012, Rev. Mike became a Certified Professional Coach by The Master Coaching Academy and Joined the Personal Empowerment Group.

Before his Metaphysical, Ministerial and Coaching studies, Rev. Mike worked for Sears Roebuck and Co. while in High School and after graduation, until he joined the U. S. Air Force in 1965. He returned to Sears from Vietnam in 1969 and stayed until 1978. His final Sears assignment was as an efficiency expert in Methods - Operational Research and Development.

He volunteered with Burholme Emergency Medical Services from 1969 and is still a Life Member and Board of Directors Member. He started a private ambulance company in 1975 and worked professionally in the field until 2001 when he devoted his full attention to real estate investing, healing, coaching, and writing.

May All Who Read This Be Blessed
AND SO IT IS!